How Clairvoyance Is Developed

C. W. Leadbeater

Kessinger Publishing's Rare Reprints

Thousands of Scarce and Hard-to-Find Books on These and other Subjects!

- Americana
- Ancient Mysteries
- Animals
- Anthropology
- Architecture
- Arts
- Astrology
- Bibliographies
- Biographies & Memoirs
- Body, Mind & Spirit
- Business & Investing
- Children & Young Adult
- Collectibles
- Comparative Religions
- Crafts & Hobbies
- Earth Sciences
- Education
- Ephemera
- Fiction
- Folklore
- Geography
- Health & Diet
- History
- Hobbies & Leisure
- Humor
- Illustrated Books
- Language & Culture
- Law
- Life Sciences
- Literature
- Medicine & Pharmacy
- Metaphysical
- Music
- Mystery & Crime
- Mythology
- Natural History
- Outdoor & Nature
- Philosophy
- Poetry
- Political Science
- Science
- Psychiatry & Psychology
- Reference
- Religion & Spiritualism
- Rhetoric
- Sacred Books
- Science Fiction
- Science & Technology
- Self-Help
- Social Sciences
- Symbolism
- Theatre & Drama
- Theology
- Travel & Explorations
- War & Military
- Women
- Yoga
- *Plus Much More!*

We kindly invite you to view our catalog list at:
http://www.kessinger.net

THIS ARTICLE WAS EXTRACTED FROM THE BOOK:

Other Side of Death Scientifically Examined and Carefully Described Part 1

BY THIS AUTHOR:

C. W. Leadbeater

ISBN 0766126080

READ MORE ABOUT THE BOOK AT OUR WEB SITE:

http://www.kessinger.net

OR ORDER THE COMPLETE
BOOK FROM YOUR FAVORITE STORE

ISBN 0766126080

CHAPTER VI

HOW CLAIRVOYANCE IS DEVELOPED

THE FIRST STEP

WHEN a man has studied the subject of clairvoyance sufficiently to realize that the claims made on its behalf are true, his next enquiry usually is: "How can I gain this power for myself? If this faculty be latent in every man, as you say, how can I so develop myself as to bring it into action, and so have direct access to all this knowledge of which you tell me?" In reply we can assure him that this thing can be done, and that it has been done. There are even many ways in which the faculty may be gained, though most of them are unsafe and eminently undesirable, and there is only one that can be thoroughly and unreservedly recommended to all men alike. That we may understand the subject, and see where lie the dangers that have to be avoided, let us consider exactly what it is that has to be done.

In the case of all cultured people belonging to the higher races of the world, the faculties of the astral body are already fully developed, as I have explained in earlier chapters. But we are not in the least in the habit of using them; they have slowly grown up within us during the ages of our evolution, but they have come to us so gradually that we have not as yet realized our powers, and they are still to a great extent untried weapons in our hands. The physical faculties, to which we are thoroughly accustomed, overshadow these others and hide their very existence, just as the nearer light of the sun hides from our eyes the light of the far-distant stars. So that there are two things to be done if we wish to enter into this part of our heritage as evolved human beings; we must keep our too insistent physical faculties out of the way for the time, and we must habituate ourselves to the employment of these others, which are as yet unfamiliar to us.

The first step, then, is to get the physical senses out of the way for the time. There are many ways of doing this, but broadly they all range themselves under two heads—one comprising methods by which they are forced out of the way by temporary violent suppression, and the other including methods, much slower but infinitely surer, by which we ourselves gain permanent control over them. Most of the methods of violent suppression are injurious to the physical body, to a greater or less extent, and they all have certain undesirable characteristics in common. One of these is that they leave the man in a passive condition, able perhaps to use his higher senses, but with little choice as to how he shall employ them, and to a large extent undefended against any unpleasant or evil influence which he may happen to encounter.

Another characteristic is that any power gained by these methods can at best be only temporary. Many of them confer it only during the limited period of their action, and even the best of them can only dower the man with certain faculties during this one physical life. In the East, where they have studied these matters for so many centuries, they divide methods of development into two classes, just as I have done, and they call them by the names *laukika* and *lokothra*, the first being the " worldly " or temporary method, any results gained by which will inhere only in the personality, and therefore be available only for this present physical life, while whatever is obtained by the second process is gained by the ego, the soul, the true man, and so is a permanent possession for evermore, carried over from one earthly life to another. For most methods of the former class little training is required, and when there is training it is of the bodies only, and so at the best it can affect only this present set of vehicles, and when the man returns into incarnation with a fresh set all his trouble will be lost ; whereas by the second method it is the soul itself which is trained in the control of its bodies, and naturally it can apply the power and the knowledge thus gained to its new vehicles in the next life. I will enumerate first some of the undesirable ways in which clairvoyance is developed in various countries.

Undesirable Methods

Among non-Aryan tribes in India it is often obtained by the use of drugs—bhang, haschish and others of the same kind. These stupefy the physical body somewhat as anæsthetics do, and thus the man in his astral vehicle is set free as he would be in sleep, but with far less possibility of being awakened. Before taking the drug, the man has set his mind strongly on the endeavour to train his astral senses into activity, and so as soon as he is free he tries to use his faculties, and with practice he succeeds to some extent. When he awakens his physical body, he remembers more or less of his visions, and tries to interpret them, and in that way he often obtains a great reputation for clairvoyance and prevision. Sometimes while in his trance some dead man may speak through him, just as might happen to any other medium. There are others who obtain the same condition by inhaling stupefying fumes, usually produced by the burning of a mixture of drugs. It is probable that the clairvoyance of the pythonesses of old was often of this type. It is stated that in the case of one of the most celebrated of those oracles of ancient days, the priestess sat always upon a tripod exactly over a crack in the rock, out of which vapour ascended. After breathing this vapour for a time, she became entranced, and some one then spoke through her organs in the ordinary way so familiar to the visitors to séances. It is not difficult for us to see how undesirable both these methods are from the point of view of real development.

Probably most of us have heard of the dancing dervishes, one part of whose religion consists in this curious dance of ecstasy, in which they whirl round and round in a kind of frenzy until vertigo seizes them, and they eventually fall insensible to the ground. In that trance, worked up as they are by religious fervour, they frequently have most extraordinary visions, and are able to some extent to experience and remember lower astral conditions. I have seen something of this, and also of the practices of the Obeah or Voodoo votaries among the negroes; but these latter are usually connected with magical ceremonies, loathsome, indecent, horrible, such as none of us would think of touching for any purpose, whatever results might be promised to us. Yet they certainly do produce effects under favourable conditions, though not such consequences as any of us could possibly wish to obtain. Indeed, none of the methods mentioned so far would at all commend themselves to us, though I have heard of Europeans who have experimented with the Oriental drugs.

Nevertheless we also have undesirable methods in the West—methods of self-hypnotization which should be carefully avoided by all who wish to develop in purity and safety. A person may be told to gaze for some time at a bright spot until paralysis of some of the brain-centres supervenes, and in that way he is cast into a condition of perfect passivity, in which it is possible that the lower astral senses may come into a measure of activity. Naturally he has no power of selection in receiving under such circumstances; he must submit himself to whatever comes in his way, good or bad—and on the whole it is much more likely to be bad than good! Sometimes the same general result is obtained by the recitation of certain formulæ, the repetition of which over and over again deadens the mental faculty almost as the gazing at a metal disc does.

Lord Tennyson's Method

It may be remembered that the poet Tennyson tells us that he was able by the recitation of his own name many times in rapid succession to pass into another condition of consciousness. The account is given in a letter in the poet's handwriting which is dated Faringford, Freshwater, Isle of Wight, May 7th, 1874. It was written to a gentleman who had communicated to him certain strange experiences he had had when passing from under the effect of anæsthetics. Lord Tennyson says:

> I have never had any revelations through anæsthetics, but a kind of waking trance (this for lack of a better name) I have frequently had, quite up from boyhood, when I have been all alone. This has often come upon me through repeating my own name to myself silently, till all at once out of the intensity of the consciousness of individuality, the individuality itself seemed to dissolve and fade away into boundless being; and this not a confused state, but the clearest of the clearest, the surest of the surest, utterly beyond words, where death was an almost laughable impossibility, the loss of personality (if so it were) seeming no extinction, but the only true life. I am ashamed of my feeble description. Have I not said that the state is utterly beyond words? This is the most emphatic declaration that the spirit of the writer is capable of transferring itself into another state of existence, is not only real, clear, simple, but that it is also infinite in vision and eternal in duration.

Here is undoubtedly a touch of the higher life; no one who has practical experience of realities can fail to recognize the description as far as it goes, even though the poet stops short just on the brink of something so infinitely grander. He seems to have held himself more positive than do many people who dabble in these matters without the necessary instruction or knowledge, and so he gained a valuable certainty of the existence of the soul apart from the body; yet even his method cannot be commended as good or really safe.

Breathing Exercises

We are sometimes told that such a faculty can be developed by means of exercises which regulate the breathing, and that this plan is one largely adopted and recommended in India. It is true that a type of clairvoyance may be developed along these lines, but too often at the cost of ruin both physical and mental. Many attempts of this sort have been made in Europe and America. This I know personally, because many who have enfeebled their constitutions, and in some cases brought themselves to the verge of insanity, have come to me to know how they could be cured. Some have succeeded in opening astral vision sufficiently to feel themselves perpetually haunted; some have not even reached that point, yet have wrecked their physical health or weakened their minds so that they are in utter despair; yet one or two declare that such practice has been beneficial to them.

It is true that such exercises are employed in India by the Hatha Yogis—those who attempt to attain development rather by physical means than by inner growth of the mental and the spiritual. But even among them such practices are used only under the direct orders of responsible teachers, who watch the effect upon the pupil of what is prescribed, and will at once stop him if the exercises prove unsuitable for him. But for people who know nothing at all of the subject to attempt such things indiscriminately is most unwise and dangerous, for the practices which are useful for one man are often disastrous for another. They may suit one man in fifty, but they are extremely likely not to suit the rest, and I myself should advise every one to abstain from them unless directed to try them by a competent teacher who really understands what they are intended to achieve. He who tries them may be the one man whom they will suit, but the probabilities are against it, for there are far more failures than successes. It is so fatally easy to do a great deal of harm in this way, that to experiment vaguely is rather like going into a chemist's shop and taking down drugs at random; we might happen to hit upon exactly what we needed, but also we might not, and the latter is many times more probable.

Mesmerism

Another method by which clairvoyance may be developed is by mesmerism—that is to say, if a person be thrown by another into a mesmeric trance it is possible that in that trance he may see astrally. The mesmerizer entirely dominates his will, and the physical faculties are thrown utterly into abeyance. That leaves the field open, and the mesmerist can at the same time stimulate the astral senses by pouring vitality into the astral body. Good results have been produced in this way, but it requires an unusual combination of circumstances, an almost superhuman development of purity in thought and intention both in the operator and the subject, to make the experiment a safe one. The mesmerist gains great influence over his subject—a far greater power than is generally known; and it may be unconsciously exercised. Any quality of heart or mind possessed by the mesmerist is readily transferred to the subject, so if he be not entirely pure, we see at once that avenues of danger open up before us. To be thrown into a trance is to give up one's individuality, and that is never a good thing in psychic experiments; but beyond and above that element of undesirability, there is real danger unless we have the highest purity of thought, word and deed in our operator; and how rarely that is to be found we all know. I should never myself submit to this process; I should never advise it to any one else.

I say nothing against the practice of curative mesmerism by those who understand it; that is a totally different matter, for in that it is unnecessary to produce the trance condition. It is perfectly possible to relieve pain, to remove disease, or to pour vitality into a man by magnetic passes, without "putting him to sleep" at all. To this there can be no possible objection; yet the man who tries to do even this much would do well to acquaint himself thoroughly with the literature of the subject, for there must always remain a certain element of danger in playing, even with the noblest intentions, with forces which the operator does not understand, which to him are still abnormal forces. None of these are plans of clairvoyant development which can be unreservedly recommended for trial by every one.

The Better Plan

What, then, it may be asked, are the desirable methods, since so many are undesirable? Broadly, those which instead of suppressing the physical body by force, train the soul to control it. The surest and safest way of all is to put oneself into the hands of a competent teacher, and practise only what he advises. But where is the qualified teacher to be found? Not, assuredly, among any who advertise themselves as teachers; not among those who take money for their instruction, and offer to sell the mysteries of the universe for so many shillings or so many dollars. Knowledge can be gained now where it has always been available—at the hands of those who are adepts in this great science of the soul, the fringe of which we are beginning to touch in our deepest studies.

There has always been a great Brotherhood of the Men who know, and They have always been ready to teach Their lore to the right man, for it is for that very purpose that They have taken the trouble to acquire it—in order that They may be able to guide and help. How can we reach Them? We cannot reach Them in the physical body, and we might not even know Them if it should happen that we saw Them. But They can reach us, and assuredly They will do so when They see us to be fit for the work of helping the world. Their one great interest is the furthering of evolution, the helping of humanity; They need men devoted to this work, and They are ever watching for them; so none need fear that he will be overlooked if he is ready for that work. They will never gratify mere curiosity; They will give no aid to one who wishes to gain powers for himself alone; but when a man has shown, by long and careful training of himself, and by using for helpfulness all the power which he already possesses, that his will is strong enough and his heart pure enough to bear his part in the Divine work—then he may become conscious of Their presence and Their aid when he least expects it.

It is true that They founded the Theosophical Society, yet membership in the Society will not of itself be sufficient to bring a man into relationship with Them—no, nor even membership in that Inner School through which the Society offers training to its more earnest members. It is true that from the ranks of the Society men have been chosen to come into closer relation with Them; but none could guarantee that as a result of becoming a member, for it rests with Them alone, for They see further into the hearts of men than we. But always be sure of this, you whose hearts are yearning for the higher life, for something greater than this lower world can give—They never overlook one honest effort, but always recognize it by giving through Their pupils such teaching and such help as is best for the man at his stage.

In the meantime, while we are trying in every way to develop ourselves along the path of progress, there is much that we can do, if we wish, to bring this power of clairvoyance nearer within our reach. Remember that it is not in itself a sign of great development; it is only one of the signs, for man has to advance along many lines simultaneously before he can reach his goal of perfection. See how highly developed is the intellect in the great scientific man; yet perhaps he may have but little of the wonderful force which devotion gives. See the splendid devotion of the great saint of some church or religion; yet in spite of all that progress along one line he may have but little of the divine power of the intellect. Each needs what the other has; each will have to acquire the faculty of the other before he will be perfect.

So it is evident that at present we are unequally developed; some have more in one direction, and some in another, according to the line along which each has worked most in past lives. If we particularly long for devotion in our character, by striving in that direction now we may attain much of it even in this life, and may assuredly make it a leading quality in our next life. So with intellect, so with every quality; so also with this faculty of clairvoyance. If you think it well to throw your strength into work along this line, you may do much towards bringing these latent faculties into action. I am not speaking here of a vague possibility, but of a definite fact, for some of our own members in this Society set themselves years ago to try to train the soul along the path of permanent progress, and of those who persevered without faltering almost every one has even already found some definite result. Some have won their faculties fully, others only partially as yet, but in all cases good has come from their efforts to take themselves in hand and control their minds and emotions.

How to Begin

If you have this desire for higher sight, take yourself in hand first in the same way; make sure first of the mental and moral development, lest you should succeed in your efforts, and gain your powers.

For to possess them without having first acquired those other qualifications would be verily a curse and not a blessing, for you would then misuse them, and your last state would indeed be worse than the first. If you consider that you have made sure of yourself, and can trust yourself under all possible circumstances to do the right for the right's sake, even against your apparent earthly interest, always to choose the utterly unselfish course of action, and to forget yourself in your love for the world, then there are at least two methods which will lead you towards clairvoyance safely, and can in no way do you harm, even though you should not succeed in your object. The first of these, though perfectly harmless and even useful, is not suited for every one; but the second is of universal application, and I have myself known both of them to be successful.

The Fourth Dimension

This first method is purely intellectual, the study of the fourth dimension of space. The physical brain has never been accustomed to act at all along those lines, and so it feels itself unable to attack such a problem. But the brain, like any other part of the physical organism, can be trained by persistent, gradual, careful effort to feats which appeared originally quite beyond its reach, and so it can be induced to understand and conceive clearly the forms of a world unlike its own. The chief apostle of the fourth dimension is Mr. C. H. Hinton, of Washington. He is not a member of our Society, but he has done many of its members an excellent piece of service in writing so clearly and luminously on his wonderful subject. In his books he tells us that he has himself succeeded in developing this power of higher conception in the physical brain, and several of our own members have followed in his footsteps.

One of these has developed astral sight simply by steadily raising the capacity of the physical brain until it contained the possibility of grasping astral form, and thus awakening the latent astral faculty proper. It is simply a question of extending the power of receptivity until it includes the astral matter. I suppose that out of a score of men who took up this effort, not more than one would succeed as well and as quickly as that; but at any rate the study is a most fascinating one for those who have a mathematical turn of mind, and where it does not bring increased faculty to see, it must at least bring wider comprehension and a broader outlook over the world; and this is no mean result, even if no other be attained. Short of absolute astral sight, it is the only method of which I know by which a clear comprehension can be gained of the appearance of astral objects, and thus a definite idea of what the astral life really is.

Another Way

If that line of effort commends itself only to the few, our second method is of universal application. It also is not easy, but its practice cannot but be of the greatest use to the man. That is its great and crowning advantage; it leads a man towards these powers which he so ardently desires; but the rate at which he can move along that road depends upon the degree of his previous development in that particular way in other lives, and therefore no one can guarantee him a certain result in a certain time; yet while he is working his way onward, every step which he takes is so far an improvement, and even though he should work for the whole of his life without winning astral sight, he would nevertheless be mentally and morally and even physically the better for having tried. This is what in various religions is called the method of meditation. For the purpose of our examination of it I shall divide it into three successive steps—concentration, meditation and contemplation; and I will explain what I mean by each of these three terms.

But remember always that to attain success, this effort must be only one side of a general development, and that it is absolutely pre-requisite for the man who would learn its secrets to live a pure and altruistic life. There is no mystery about the rules of the greater progress; the Steps of the Path of

Holiness have been known to the world for ages; the clearest and simplest statement of them is given in that beautiful little book *At the Feet of the Master*, and I have myself written of them in *The Masters and the Path*. There is no difficulty in knowing what to do; the difficulty is in carrying out the directions which all religions have given.

Concentration

The first step necessary towards the attainment of the higher clairvoyance is concentration—not to gaze at a bright spot until you have no mind left, but to acquire such control over your mind that you can do with it what you will, and fix it exactly where you want to hold it for as long a period as you choose. This is not an easy task; it is one of the most difficult and arduous known to man; but it can be done, because it has been done—not once, but hundreds of times, by those whose will is strong and immovable. There may be some among us who have never thought how much beyond our control our minds usually are. Stop yourself suddenly when you are walking along the street, or when you are riding in your car, and see what you are thinking, and why. Try to follow the thought back to its genesis, and you will probably be surprised to find how many desultory thoughts have wandered through your brain during the previous five minutes, just dropping in and dropping out again, and leaving almost no impression. You will gradually begin to realize that in truth all these are not your thoughts at all, but simply cast-off fragments of other people's thoughts.

The fact is that thought is a force, and every exertion of it leaves an impression behind. A strong thought about some other person goes to him, a strong thought of self clings about the thinker; but many thoughts are not by any means strong or especially pointed in any direction, and so the forms which they create are vaguely-floating and evanescent. While they last they are capable of entering into any mind that happens to come their way, and so it comes that as we walk along the road we leave a trail of feeble thought behind us, and the next man who passes that way finds these valueless fragments intruding themselves upon his consciousness. They drift into his mind, unless it is already occupied with something definite, and in the majority of cases they just drift out again, having made only the most trifling impression upon his brain; but here and there he encounters one which interests or pleases him, and then he takes that up and turns it over in his mind, so that it departs from him somewhat strengthened by the addition of a little of his mind-force to it. He has made it his own thought for a moment, and so has coloured it with his personality. Every time we enter a room we step into the midst of a crowd of thoughts, good, bad or indifferent as the case may be, but the great mass of them just a dull, purposeless fog which is hardly worth calling thought at all.

If we wish to develop any higher faculty, we must begin by gaining control over this mind of ours. We must give it some work to do, instead of just letting it play about as it will, drawing into itself all these thoughts which are not ours, which we really do not want at all. It must not be our master but our servant before we can take the first step along the line of the true trained clairvoyance, for this is the instrument which we shall have to use, and it must be at our command and fully under our control.

This concentration is one of the hardest things for the ordinary man to do, because he has had no practice in it, and indeed has scarcely realized that it needed to be done. Think what it would be if your hand were as little under your control as your mind is, if it did not obey your command, but started aside from what you wished it to do. You would feel that you had paralysis, and that your hand was useless. But if you cannot control your mind, that is dangerously like a mental paralysis; you must practise with it until you have it in hand and can use it as you wish. Fortunately concentration can be practised all day long, in the common affairs of every-day life. Whatever you are doing, do it thoroughly, and keep your mind on it. If you are writing a letter, think of your letter and of nothing else until it is finished; it will be all the better written for such care. If you are reading a book, fix your mind on it and try to grasp the author's full meaning. Know always what you are thinking about, and why; keep your mind at intelligent work, and do not leave it time to be idle, for it is in those idle moments that all evil comes.

Even now you can concentrate perfectly when your interest is sufficiently keenly excited. Then your mind is so entirely absorbed that you hardly hear what is said to you, or see what passes round you.

The Courtiers and the Water-Jars

There is a story told in the East about some sceptical courtiers, who declined to believe that an ascetic could ever be so occupied with his meditation as to be unaware that an army passed close by him as he sat under his tree rapt in thought. The sultan, who was present, assured them that he would prove to them the possibility of this, and proceeded to do so in a truly Oriental and autocratic way. He ordered that some large water-jars should be brought and filled to the brim. Then he instructed the courtiers each to take one and carry it; and his command was that they should walk, carrying this water, through the principal streets of the city. But they were to be surrounded by his guards with drawn swords, and if one of them spilled one single drop of his water, that unfortunate was to be instantly beheaded then and there. The courtiers started on their journey filled with terror; but they all came safely back again, and the sultan smilingly greeted them with a request to tell him all the incidents of their walk, and describe the persons whom they had met. Not one of them could mention even one person that they had seen, for all agreed that they had been so entirely occupied with the one idea of watching the brimming jars that they had noticed nothing else of any sort. "So, gentlemen," rejoined the sultan, "you see that when there is sufficient interest concentration is possible."

Meditation

When you have attained concentration such as that, not under the stress of the fear of instant death, but by the exertion of your will, then you may profitably try the next stage of effort. I do not say that it will be easy; on the contrary, it is very difficult; but it can be done, for many of us have had to do it. When your mind is thus an instrument, try what we call meditation. Choose a certain fixed time for yourself, when you can be undisturbed; the early morning is in many ways the best, if that can be managed. It is not always an easy time for us now, for we have in modern civilization hopelessly disarranged our day, so that noon is no longer its middle point, as it should be. Now we lie in bed long after the sun has risen, and then stay up injuring our eyes with artificial light long after he has set at night. But choose your time, and let it be the same time each day, and let no day pass without your regular effort. We know, if we are trying any sort of physical exercise for training purposes, how much more effective it is to do a little regularly than to make a violent effort one day, and then to do nothing for a week. So in this matter it is the regularity that is important.

Sit down comfortably where you will not be disturbed, and turn your mind, with all its newly-developed power of concentration, upon some selected subject demanding high and useful thought. We in our Theosophical studies have no lack of such subjects, combining deepest interest with greatest profit. If you prefer it you can take some moral quality, as is advised by the Catholic Church when it prescribes this exercise. In that case, you will turn the quality over in your mind, see how it is an essential quality in the Divine order, how it is manifested in Nature about you, how it has been shown forth by great men of old, how you yourself can manifest it in your daily life, how (perhaps) you have failed to display it in the past, and so on. Such meditation upon a high moral quality is a good exercise in many ways, for it not only trains the mind, but keeps the good thought constantly before you. But it needs to be preceded generally by thought upon concrete subjects, and when those are easy for you, you can usefully take up the more abstract ideas.

When this has become an established habit with you, with which nothing is allowed to interfere; when you can manage it fairly well without any feeling of strain or difficulty, and without a single wandering thought ever venturing to intrude itself, then you may turn to the third stage of our effort—contemplation. But remember that you will not succeed with this until you have entirely conquered the mind-wandering. For a long time you will find, when you try to meditate, that your thoughts are continually going off at a tangent, and you do not know it till suddenly you start to find how far away they have gone. You must not let this dishearten you, for it is the common experience; you must simply bring the errant mind back again to its duty, a hundred or a thousand times if necessary, for the only way to succeed is to decline to admit the possibility of failure. But when you have at length succeeded, and the mind is definitely mastered, then we reach that for which all the rest has been but the necessary preparation, good though it has been in itself.

CONTEMPLATION

Instead of turning over a quality in your mind, take the highest spiritual ideal that you know. It does not matter what it is, or by what name you call it. A Theosophist will most probably take one of those Great Ones to whom we have already referred—a member of that great Brotherhood of Adepts whom we call the Masters—especially if he has the privilege of having come directly into contact with one of them. The Catholic may take the Blessed Virgin or some patron saint, the ordinary Christian will probably take the Christ; the Hindu will perhaps choose Shri Krishna, and the Buddhist most likely the Lord Buddha Himself. Names do not matter, for we are dealing with realities now. But it must be to you the highest, that which will evoke in you the greatest feeling of reverence, love and devotion that you are capable of experiencing. In place of your previous meditation, call up the most vivid mental image that you can make of this ideal, and, letting your most intense feeling go out towards this highest One, try with all the strength of your nature to raise yourself towards Him, to become one with Him, to be in and of that glory and beauty. If you will do that, if you will thus steadily continue to raise your consciousness, there will come a time when you will suddenly find that you are one with that ideal as you never were before, when you realize and understand Him as you never did before, for a new and wonderful light has somehow dawned for you, and all the world has changed, for now for the first time you know what it is to live, and all life before seems like darkness and death to you as compared with this.

Then it will all slip away again, and you will return to the light of common day—and darkness indeed will it appear by comparison! But go on working at your contemplation, and presently that glorious moment will come again and yet again; and each time it will stay with you longer, till there comes a period when that higher life is yours always, no longer a flash or a glimpse of paradise, but a steady glow, a new and never-ceasing marvel every day of your existence. Then for you day and night will be one continuous consciousness, one beautiful life of happy work for the helping of others; yet this, which seems so indescribable and so unsurpassable, is only the beginning of the entrance into the heritage in store for you and for every child of man. Look about you with that new and higher sight, and you will see and grasp many things which until now you have never even suspected—unless, indeed, you have previously familiarized yourself with the investigations of your predecessors along this path.

Continue your efforts, and you will rise higher still, and in due course there will open before your astonished eyes a life as much grander than the astral as that is than the physical, and once more you will feel that the true life has been unknown to you until now; for all the while you are rising nearer to the One Life which alone is perfect Truth and perfect Beauty.

This is a development that must take years, you will say. Yes, that is probable, for you are trying to compress into one life the evolution which would normally spread itself over many; but it is far more than worth the time and the effort. No man can say how long it will take in any individual case, for that depends upon two things—the amount of crust that there is to break through, and the energy and determination that is put into the work. I cannot promise you that in so many years you will certainly succeed; I can only tell you that many have tried before you, and that many have succeeded. All the great Masters of Wisdom were once men at our own level; as They have risen, so must we rise. Many of us in our humbler way have tried also, and have succeeded, some more and some less; but none who has tried regrets his attempt, for whatever he has gained, be it little or much, is gained for all eternity, since it inheres in the soul which survives death. Whatever we gain thus we possess in full power and consciousness, and have it always at our command; for this is no mediumship, no feeble intermittent trance-quality, but the power of the developed and glorified life which is to be that of all humanity some day.

Pre-requisites

But the man who wishes to try to unfold these faculties within himself will be ill-advised if he does not take care first of all to have utter purity of heart and soul, for that is the first and greatest necessity. If he is to do this, and to do it well, he must purify the mental, the astral and the physical; he must cast aside his pet vices and his physical impurities; he must cease to defile his body with meat, with alcohol or tobacco, and try to make himself pure and clean all through, on this lower plane as well as on the higher. If he does not think it worth while to give up petty uncleannesses for the higher life, that is exclusively his own affair; it was said of old that one cannot serve God and Mammon simultaneously. I do not say that bad habits on the physical plane will prevent him altogether from any psychic development, but I do emphatically and distinctly say that the man who remains unclean is never free from danger, and that to touch holy things with impure hands is to risk a terrible peril.

The man who would try for the higher must free his mind from worry and from lower cares; while doing his duty to the uttermost, he must do it impersonally and for the right's sake, and leave the result in the hands of higher powers. So will he draw round him pure and helpful entities as he moves onward, and will himself radiate sunlight on those in suffering or in sorrow. So shall he remain master of himself, pure and clean and unselfish, using his new powers never for a personal end, but ever for the advancement and the succour of men his brothers, that they also, as they can, may learn to live the wider life, may learn to rise from amid the mists of ignorance and selfishness into the glorious sunlight of the peace of God.

Take up this study of Theosophy then, not on blind faith—for blind faith has done enough harm in the world already—but for enquiry; if you are not satisfied, there is no harm done, while if you are satisfied, much good may come to you thereby, as it has come to the rest of us. The best way of all to see whether this thing is so, is to act as if it were true; live the life which it teaches, and note its effects. Try the thought-control which it recommends, and see whether you are the better or the worse for it. Try to realize the unity and brotherhood which it teaches, and to show the unselfishness which it exacts; and then see for yourself whether this is an improvement upon other modes of living or not. It still remains true now, as in days of old, that they that do the will of the Father that is in heaven, they shall know of the doctrine, whether it be true.

The surest way to find the truth is to live the life; try the unselfishness and the watchful helpfulness, and see whether here is not an opening into new fields of happiness and usefulness. From that go on gradually to other parts of the teaching, and you will find evidence enough. Think what the world would be if all held these doctrines of the fatherhood of God and the brotherhood of man; would it be better, or would it be worse, if all mankind held unity as a fact, and unselfishness as a duty? As yet we are only at the beginning of this mightiest of studies; yet we say to you with utmost confidence: Come and join us in our study, and to you also will come the peace and confidence that has come to us, so that through your study of Theosophy your lives shall become happier to yourselves and more useful to your fellow-men.

This is the end of this publication.

Any remaining blank pages are for our book binding requirements and are blank on purpose.

To search thousands of interesting publications like this one, please remember to visit our website at:

http://www.kessinger.net

CPSIA information can be obtained
at www.ICGtesting.com
Printed in the USA
BVHW070602310520
580408BV00003B/269